First Printing, 2025.

ISBN: 978-1-951573-62-1

www.educatelearners.com

We use money to buy things we want and need.

There are
different kinds
of money.

This type of money is called coins.

This type of money is called paper money.

Coins are worth
less than a dollar.

Paper money is worth a dollar or more.

This is a penny.
A penny is a coin.

$0.01

One penny is
worth 1 cent.

$0.05

Five pennies are
worth 5 cents.

This is a nickel.
A nickel is a coin.

$0.05

A nickel is
worth 5 cents.

$0.10

Two nickels are
worth 10 cents.

This is a dime.
A dime is a coin.

$0.10

A dime is
worth 10 cents.

$0.50

Five dimes are
worth 50 cents.

This is a quarter.
A quarter is a coin.

$0.25

A quarter is
worth 25 cents.

$1.00

Four quarters are
worth 1 dollar.

Coins can add up to a dollar amount

100 pennies = $1.00

20 nickels = $1.00

10 dimes = $1.00

4 quarters = $1.00

Paper money is different amounts of a dollar bill

1 dollar bill = $1.00

5 dollar bills = $5.00

10 dollar bills = $10.00

20 dollar bills = $20.00

50 dollar bills = $50.00

100 dollar bills = $100.00

This is a dollar bill.

A dollar bill is paper money.

$1.00

A dollar bill is worth 1 dollar.

This is a five dollar bill.

A five dollar bill is paper money.

$5.00

A five dollar bill is worth 5 dollars.

This is a ten dollar bill.

A ten dollar bill is paper money.

$10.00

A ten dollar bill is
worth 10 dollars.

This is a
twenty dollar bill.

A twenty dollar bill is
paper money.

$20.00

A twenty dollar bill is worth 20 dollars.

This is a fifty dollar bill.

A fifty dollar bill is paper money.

$50.00

A fifty dollar bill is worth 50 dollars.

This is a
one hundred dollar bill.

A one hundred dollar
bill is paper money.

$100.00

A one hundred
dollar bill is
worth 100 dollars.

THANK YOU FOR READING!

Get a free year long subscription to our online education resource library when you purchase any one of our books.

Code: EDBOOKS

educatelearners.com